P9-DBT-419

At the Airport

Grateful Acknowledgement is made to

James Luce
Department of the Treasury
United States Customs Service

Judith E. Hamill
Program Director
Department of Aviation

Design and Art Direction
Lindaanne Donohoe Design

Illustrations
Penny Dann

● ● ● ● ● ● ● ● ● ● ● ● ● ●

Library of Congress Cataloging-in-Publication Data

Greene, Carol.

At the airport/by Carol Greene.
p.   cm.
Summary: Describes the things seen at an airport and
explains the activities of people who work there.
ISBN 1-56766-292-7 (smythe-sewn library reinforced: alk. paper)
1. Airports — Juvenile literature. 2. Air travel — Juvenile literature.
[1. Airports. 2. Air travel.] I. Title.

TL725.G68   1998   97-900
387.7'36—dc21   CIP
                                                        AC

At the Airport

By Carol Greene
Photographs by Phil Martin

The Child's World®

WHOOSH!   WHOOSH!
RRRROAR!

It is noisy outside the airport.

Noisy in the sky and noisy on the ground.

It is noisy inside the airport too.
People line up at the check-in desk.
They leave their baggage there.
Workers make sure each person
gets to the right plane.

Some airports
have more than
one building!

Each building is called a terminal.
Passengers must walk through
a security check before they board a plane.
Machines and people make sure no one
is carrying anything dangerous.

Security checks protect everyone.

TAP! TAP! TAP! CLOMP! CLOMP!
People of all ages and sizes hurry
down the concourse to their planes.
Special doors, called gates, line each
side of the concourse. Each gate
has a special number.

People who need
help can ride
a wheelchair or
a special car.

Outside each gate is a place for the plane to park. Inside is a waiting area for the passengers.

Up in the control tower, traffic controllers
talk to the pilots by radio. They tell
them how to land and take off in order.
"Flight 279, you are cleared for landing
on Runway 2," says a controller.

Everyone's safety depends on those controllers.

E E E E E E E!

The pilot slows the plane down

and comes in for a landing.

On the ground pilots reverse the jet engines so the plane can slow down quickly.

THUMP! THUMP! THUMP!

The plane moves slowly to the gate.

The ground crew rush out to help the pilot.

Parking this huge plane is tricky.

Ground crews push steps out to some planes so the passengers can get off. Other planes use a kind of tunnel called a jetway. One end of the jetway is attached to the plane's door. The other end opens right into the airport.

Jetways are great in bad weather.

THUD! THUD! PLOP!

Here comes the baggage off the plane.

It will go to the baggage-claim area.

Passengers come here to pick up their baggage.

It is a good idea to lock your suitcase so it does not pop open.

Passengers arriving from other countries must go through Customs. Customs officials check each person. They ask each one why they are coming into the country. Are they going to work? Or are they here to visit?

Sometimes customs officials look into your baggage.

Custom officials also make sure people
do not bring anything illegal into the country.
This dog is looking for drugs.

It is time for Flight 444 to take off.

A truck pushes the plane away from the gate.

The pilot taxis the plane to its runway.
Soon the control tower radios,
"Flight 444, you are cleared for takeoff."

Have a good trip!!

Glossary

baggage—suitcases, boxes, and bags that people carry when they travel

claim area—place at the airport where people pickup their baggage

concourse—wide passage

control tower—tall building that houses the people and machines that guide pilots and their planes in and out of an airport

custom officials—people who work for the government check the people and baggage that come into a country

drugs—substances that change physical or mental conditions in the human body

gate—place where airplanes park at the airport

ground crew—the people who work on planes before take off and after landing

illegal—against the law

jetway—name for the walkway that leads passengers onto the plane

runway—long, flat, straight path that is built for planes to land on and take off

passengers—people who pay money to ride on a plane, train, bus, or boat

pilots—people who are trained to fly planes

radio—instrument that can send and receive sound waves through the air

security check—place where people and bags are looked at to make sure no dangerous things are carried

terminal—building where people go to get on their plane

traffic controllers—people who guide planes in and out of an airport safely

About the Author
Carol Greene has written over 200 books for children. She also likes to read books, make teddy bears, work in her garden, and sing. Ms. Greene lives in Webster Groves, Missouri.